WHERE THE MONARCHS NEVER DIE

Poems by Rocío Franco

ARCANA
POETRY PRESS

For my beloved ancestor Graciela Franco,
siempre la recordaré con mucho cariño,

For Chicago's immigrant and migrant
communities. This city is yours, too.

For Rolando and Iliana,
always my home.

CONTENTS

01. WHERE THE MONARCHS NEVER DIE

02. WORKER'S ELEGY

05. FIVE-YEAR-OLD CHILD

06. HOW I EXPLAIN GENTRIFICATION TO MY DAUGHTER

07. SMILE STREET

09. WHERE THE MONARCHS NEVER DIE

10. DREAMING OF THE 'BURBS

12. A SATURDAY AFTERNOON IN OUR URBAN LANDSCAPE

13. EL 4 DE JULIO

14. WHERE THE MONARCHS NEVER DIE

15. CITY OF BROAD SHOULDERS 2024

18. WITCHES & SPIRITS

19. MCDONALD'S ON CERMAK AND WESTERN

22. TASTE OF CHICAGO

25. LA MARIPOSA MONARCA MAKES A LIST OF PLACES TO VISIT IN CHICAGO

27. IN THE '90s, WE COULDN'T AFFORD TO GO TO A BULLS' GAME

28. WHEN I THINK OF YOU

30. WHEN YOUR GIRLS MAKE IT

32. CHICAGO TO LA TO CHICAGO

WHERE THE MONARCHS NEVER DIE
📍 *Morelia, México*

We stab eggs under arches the spanish built,
admire how blood can build something beautiful.
My new friend and I wobble in our chairs
as our wounds peek out.
Hers settle around her shoulders like a rebozo.
Mine sit within my cells battered and beaten by cancer.
Wounds, if poked, will bleed and blend
with the stones beneath our feet.
The waiter brings out las conchas
that don't compare
to the ones consumed in the north
When the café de olla arrives, we broach on.
Where were you born?
What brings you here?
How did you meet so and so?
As I bite into my runny egg,
words spill out of her mouth
and land on my plate.
My father and son drowned not too long ago.
I nod and purse my lips—nothing
I say will bring her solace.
How does someone survive
two losses of this magnitude?

1

WORKER'S ELEGY

Chicago, u.s.a.

they say read theory,
research the industrial complex,
hang with the 2 lions posted up
at the art institute,
but all I can do
is read the single digit
on the ATM screen,
can't even afford the beer can
that rattles down the sidewalk,
the wind kicks it away
from streets layered with ash,
where I learned to tuck the gold chain
I inherited from my immigrant parents,
they hoped I would triple it,
show my daughter that I built generational wealth,
but I have to guard my investment,
look over my shoulder,
ready to sprawl
in case bullets decide to dance,
and speaking of dance,
the bosses love to waltz around the low wages they dump
into my account every 2 weeks,
they tell us good employees eat pizza
to earn their way to heaven, sometimes
I wish cancer would have finished its business,
because then my hospital bills would live on
without me,
a friend told me once that her dead husband
has better credit now than when he lived,

2

we both started laughing,
why mourn our circumstances without a sense of humor,
one thing they can't take away from me
is how I carry each small catastrophe,
how I walk and walk to cope,
to escape into the bit of nature
this city squeezes between
million dollar developments,
gentrified galleries glare at me,
for a moment
I'm canvassed on their glass doors,
I'm a work of art
if I stand there long enough
for them to see my value,
a tissue paper with red polka dots
passes over my head,
its flit and flutter feels in sync
with max richter's vladimir's blues,
I like classical music enough
to appreciate the thrum
of string instruments,
there's a soothing that comes from
the strum of strings,
it reminds me I can compose music
with my hair if I try hard enough,
and they always say try harder,
work harder, pull out your teeth
so you eat less,
start a mutual fund
with your morning coffee savings,

maybe one day you'll have enough
to take a vacation in a gutter,
buy a one-room condo,
grow vegetables in a one-inch garden,
don't get me wrong,
I want to read theory
research the industrial complex
peruse old immaculate hallways
with my 2 lion homies,
but I have to work this weekend,
and pull double shifts all next week.

FIVE-YEAR-OLD CHILD

Monday:

Across the iron bridge,
Cookie Monster's blue plush
smushes against your small body.
Passing semis make the bridge wobble,
your mother holds on tighter.

Tuesday:

At the 21 Cermak bus stop, a red school bag
rests on your back. You've slept
on a cold cot all night. The white man
I work with, the one with a warm apartment,
jeers, "those migrants."

Wednesday:

The river under the iron bridge sparkles
winter sun. You skim pebbles across it,
giggle at the brief indents
they leave in the water. Your eyes go wide
as they sink slowly to the bottom.

Thursday:

You shiver in the December wind.
Your Paw Patrol jacket, gloves,
and hat are barely enough.
You walk ahead of your father and mother—
you disappear around the corner.

HOW I EXPLAIN GENTRIFICATION
TO MY DAUGHTER

We walk down 18th Street and observe a flock of vultures
deep in the cavity of a *recovered wasteland.*
Now an area with charm, culture, and palatable tacos.

18th Street was rough like bricks in rubble,
blocks hot to the touch, streets buried in divestment,
big-city neglect. Chicago allows us to cocoon

in our hoods until they metamorphose into neighborhoods.
Property emerging cheap to turn into a gallery, brewery, or
some fusion bullshit. Those vultures who now flock *safely*

will never understand how I found Love as I sat
on a tuft of brown grass in Harrison Park.
How the paletero signaled summer with his cartful

of rainbows, how fire hydrant waves were our only way
to swim. How my favorite taquería introduced me to tongue.
That it can be savored, not something they peck into silence.

Our home was never a wasteland. This is sacred ground
full of swift-hand migrants and first-gen hustlers
who refuse to be displaced or gorged on like prey.

SMILE STREET

I walk a cold Chicago block.
All the homes are paint-chipped
brown, gray, and white.
A neighbor burns wood nearby,
the smell of smoke fuses—

to the memories of my abuelita's pueblo in México.
To the fogón where she pats masa
between sun-kissed hands,
forms tortillas to bless the black comal
(*un altar para el maíz*).
Thin brown branches burn at its base.
Finally the first tortilla puffs, and it's ready
to be dressed in salsa y frijoles—

on my neighbor's roof,
a black shingle flaps.
The wind has puffed it loose. But—

I'm beckoned to the tortilla—
whose burnt edges wait to land on my tongue.
The church campanas en la plaza clang
against the horizon.
Each toll echoes through orange,
yellow, and turquoise homes.
The doors and windows swing open
as stars blink in the sky—

and the crunch of my boots
under dog-piss snow brings me back
to dull homes shadowed in big city silence—

there are cities full of streets where lives fold into gravel,
but there are also corners that deserve to be
unburied and exalted,
like my abuelita's pueblo where color resists
the blood in the cobblestones—

the neighbor extinguishes the flames,
and the ashes swirl in the wind.
When I reach the end of the block
and look down at my boots,
there is a smile carved into the concrete.
For now, this is enough.

WHERE THE MONARCHS NEVER DIE

Sierra Chincua, Butterfly Sanctuary, México

Bound together by grief, we finish breakfast and leave to chase las mariposas Monarca. It's a four-hour trip from Morelia to las montañas, where the Monarcas rest on Oyamel trees for the winter. The tour guide goes on and on about the u.s. and canada owning most of the mines we pass on the way to the highlands. We're not surprised by this. Colonization courses through the veins of este país. Ransacking resources is like sport, like football—two bloody u.s. pastimes.

We arrive at our destination, and immediately there's an electric energy fluttering around us. Our trek to the Monarcas is an additional hour's hike by land or horse. The terrain is rocky and mud-thick, and the path is narrow. At one point, we are single-file, inches from the edge of the mountainside. The breeze can sweep us into the mountain's green canopy—if it feels mischievous enough.

After some time, we see a few mariposas gliding between the branches of the Oyamel. Suddenly, it bursts orange, black, and white. There are thousands upon thousands of mariposas flying about. If we get too close, they can pull us into their four-wing funnel. Our jaws drop to the dirt at this barely describable sight. How generous nature can be to help us carry our grief.

DREAMING OF THE 'BURBS

Chicago, u.s.a. | *for my beloved Rolando*

We dream of quiet paved roads,
wrap-around porches, the Smiths
knocking, bearing pies. We hatch
American dreams in our twin bed,

no air conditioning, McDonald's dinner,
hot box cable crouched away from windows
until bullets pass. Holes in the drywall
are immersive art, frustration, portals.

You display your love in ink, graffiti,
mix tapes. Wield magic for me to stay.
You are more than what they did to you.
I rail against you at first. I always

teeter with a knife between my lips
and razors to my wrists.
You pressed my palms against your chest
to keep them still. Kiss my shoulder

to calm me. You say you'll never leave,
and you haven't. During each storm, you
make me rumble with laughter. Throw
my head back, open mouth, teeth

toward the sky type of joy. Mini van, barbecue
every summer Saturday, soft rock playing
from an old CD player will never be us.
We're steady chaotic city love. Ratty couch-sitting,

electric rail riding to downtown job kind
of love. Scraping together stardust
and pennies to make something out
of nothing love. We continue to survive beyond

what they said. Don't need to dust off
our vows because everywhere we go
there is a light that never goes out.

A SATURDAY AFTERNOON
IN OUR URBAN LANDSCAPE

                i am
in a small backyard
made of concrete &   soil
with the first people
that showed me

                love

más agua que sangre   it's steamy outside   over 90 degrees
& the sun is bearing down on us   mi cuñado grills chorizo
on an old rusty garbage can   with a steel grate on top
my nieces & nephews jump   in & out of old tires
a jumble of giggles   the youngest   picks a stick
to draw some abstraction   in the dirt   while the adults sit
on milk crates & rusty chairs   we are here   for no particular
reason   other than to celebrate the weekend
& the simplicity that poverty brings   there is not much
to marvel   but we are tribe   each having survived
our own personal slaughters

12

EL 4 DE JULIO

is a day to smell
arrachera sizzling
on a corroded
grate caked in grind
while 13 coronas sweat
on a glass table splashed
with blood red salsa.
The only reminder
of colonial power
is the formation
of hotdogs and burgers
caked in american cheese.
The chatter of English
intermingled
with *dame una cerveza*
as the pool splashes
means we can afford
the water bill.
The crack of 50 peonies
set the sky on fire.
We are harmony
to their dissonance.
A family of bruised warriors
whose independence
is this backyard
and the laughter
that didn't surrender
to red, white, and blue

WHERE THE MONARCHS NEVER DIE

Wings carry mothers and fathers
across deserts and rivers
where they'll exchange labor
for their child's wild dreams. To build
a life from concrete sidewalks,
vacant lots bursting with milkweed,
and fickle seasons.

The bosses will always breathe
down the migrant's neck.
Forget you were descendants of warriors
who farmed maiz, frijoles, tomates.
Remember that we conquered you
and ransacked your lands.

But migrants, like the monarca, spread their wings
to show the bosses that borders are imaginary.

And when they say go back,
We say *Abolish Ice.*

And when they say *this is not your home,*
We say *Abolish Borders.*

And when they say *speak English,*
We say *Chinga tu Migra.*

CITY OF BROAD SHOULDERS 2024

I.

The stench of burnt asphalt fills my nostrils,
as does the dust from the buildings this city
razes to build corporate glass houses
for corporate zombies. They knock down
churches and remake them into condos
for the suburban birds to fly back to.
The priest said that the house of the lord is sacred,
but he forgot to leave out
how the presidents in our pockets are holier.
Everything can be sold and bought on the mag mile,
especially the machine politicians. They grease
their heels to slide away from the messes they make.
The lines keep bleeding after all this time,
like that boy across the street who laid down his life
for a hand gesture and a promise of a family—
The pole on the corner is a revolving funeral marker,
and this city, this city burns every day outside my window.
Sometimes, it's a metaphor
that hasn't been fully fleshed out.
Sometimes, the smoke speaks for itself.

Quiet here is dangerous. The sirens
have become a symphony that we
hum along to. What are we without
the concrete and the trees that remind
us that something beautiful can
grow from a hard gray surface?

But we can never get too comfortable,
or trust the spring when it arrives.
Warmer weather brings bullets,
and the news makes me weary.
The mothers, the mothers are
not guaranteed their children.

Have you seen the new development?
Homes worth a million dollars are built
on land that has been taken over and over.
Their children will be safe, and ours will be sacrificed.

II.

Between two run-down graffitied buildings,
the grand tower keeps being renamed but
holds the same meaning. We can worship
from afar, but your entry is at the behest
of tailored suits and polished shoes.

There are a few things to love about this city.
Ms. Gwendolyn said *We real cool.* We—
don't owe them upscale or respectability.
The basketball court holds our sweat,
and the corners sizzle with meat.
The children run around with red tongues
and sticky fingers.

The only reason *We*
smooth these streets is for dusty gym shoes
to run towards the horizon,
not away from teeth-baring badges
We want them to know our children are golden and free.

The gold coast is too gaudy to own
the lake that survived fire after fire.
The only things I want to burn are the
buildings that scrape the sky. I want
to free the land and inch the border
into oblivion. The border is what
my parents crossed to defrost
their dreams, but they didn't know
how cold January could get. How
you can't feel your toes and fingers
at the bus stop, and the smoke coming
out of your mouth reminds us how
far we are from the warm pyramids
of our ancestors. Would they
have wanted this for us? Fighting to make
a few dollars to buy a few bricks to keep
our baubles shiny. This city—this city—cannot
turn into ash. Our children
need to stretch beyond the pyre.

WITCHES & SPIRITS

The

liquor store

on 35th & Western

is occupied by witches & spirits.

Zombielike men arrive every friday

to relieve the stress of the work week.

The system's oppressions eat away at their

cerebrums, leaving no trace of resistance. Witches

gather around the men & call out their misogynistic

horrors. They cast a spell to unburden them of

their power. These men will no longer burn

the incantations of our collective hour.

MCDONALD'S ON CERMAK AND WESTERN

I'm too old to eat like this, but
sometimes, I still take the risk.
Big Macs are for young stomachs.
Once you're in your 40's,
it sits in your gut like a brick.

I almost regret this risk
until I hear the retired men toss
around their hot potato exploits,
the land they left in Mexico,
the dream house
they never finished building.

A dollar cup of coffee sits
in their gnarled, vein-bumped hands.
Apple pie dust mingles
with their gray-peppered beards.

A woman with weather-stamped skin
talks to her dreams in a corner booth.
When she walks, she scrapes out
little stories from her cracked soles.

Kids trample around
in their black-bottomed socks.
They run from the tunnel slide
to their cold nuggets and fries.

When I was their age,
large cartoon hamburgers
sat outside. I tunneled through them—
the fake grass damp and rough
against my five-year-old knees and palms.
They were caves, and I hid from dangers
I didn't quite understand yet.

I take my daughter here now.
It's not the same though.
They've replaced workers with screens.
A few years ago, the fight for fifteen
felt ridiculous to those who respect
a suit and skirt type of work
over
a beef and potato type of work.

Why shouldn't these workers make a living wage?
They've helped shape modern society.
McDonald's on Cermak and Western
holds sorrows, expired dreams,
warmth during winter.

Big Macs that sit like bricks in aging stomachs,
fries that don't taste the same
as when I was five. They deserve to make
fifty dollars an hour, as far as I'm concerned.

Because I've learned how the world revolves
around the dollar.

Buns and starch raise my sugar, my pressure
takes a hit from all the sodium, and the cash
remains at the top in piles I contribute to.
But I return, even though the grease
rebels in my guts every single time.

TASTE OF CHICAGO

It doesn't take long to get ready
when the job trades tickets for tacos.
To decide on clothes where the oil won't show.
You pluck your blackest T-shirt from the closet
so you can mask the yellow in your armpits.
Memory foam your feet for all the hours
you'll stand in front of a hungry crowd.
Subtract a half hour for lunch, where you'll sit
in a milk crate corner that suffocates you
with two kinds of heat. You'll eat the tacos de asada
that come with your shift. The red rash that creeps
up your legs will keep you entertained.
You don't know how much you can sweat
until a grease griddle sizzles three kinds of meat
inches from your back.

Taqueros with glistening skin
scoop exact mounds onto double tortillas.
They dress them like fashionistas
for the whole city to devour.
Cebolla and cilantro or lettuce and tomato—
it's all good in the hood here.
You turn so much from grill to crowd
that you become a wood-spinning pirinola.
You dispatch little red and white boats
without a morsel abandoning their ships.
Spin and spin and spin;
you spin for all nine and a half hours.
The glistening men call you

a taco dispatching ballerina.
But your legs have no grace
after they swell from the swelter.
It's a stale ninety-five degrees
with a food stall factor of a hundred and ten.

But you're proud of working hard
under grueling conditions.
It's the American way.
You've inherited your papi's work ethic.
You've learned to earn your existence
in between better-paying jobs.
You survive what the city and sun can give.

Dusk settles in, and the taqueros whistle
and talk about the beer they'll chug
despues del jale.
It's also the American way
to drink ourselves from one shift to the next.

The crowds diminish.
They go home with
morsels of Chicago
in their stomachs. You walk
to the train station with a heat rash
that creeps up your thighs.

Three kinds of meat
have penetrated your skin.
Tomorrow, you'll be back
for more sizzle and sweat.
As you climb the stairs to the platform,
your feet want to flee the memory foam.
You want to set your clothes on fire
to forget the smell.

LA MARIPOSA MONARCA MAKES A LIST
OF PLACES TO VISIT IN CHICAGO

faded murals on 16th street; stories of ancestors past

where the basketball bounces to the beat of car boosted bass

corner store where the hood kids buy their hot chips
and gatorade

weeds on the neglected corner where another child
was murdered

school that closed because it was on the city's redline

el taquero on Western & 33rd that hustles to get by

not that bean sculpture or tower that tourist traps the rich

the pizza spot where they sell cheap slices; can't afford
deep dish

el supermercado where the meat is okay, the fruit
is bruised, but they take SNAP

gold coast so I can show them beauty they can't buy

da club where they play Freestyle, House, & the dancing
never stops

el elotero that scoops corn into a cup to send money back
to México

the projects they turned into mixed income households

nope, not that newly gentrified neighborhood

the lake that brings everyone together in the summer

church where the women bond over whispers

parks where the Black & Brown kids play

where hope never perishes even when winter arrives, & I fly
away

IN THE '90s, WE COULDN'T AFFORD TO GO TO A BULLS' GAME

for my beloved Rolando

Next to their jail cell, we dribbled in our high school gym—

fade-away jumpers into fade-away dreams.

The girls would post up against boastful boys

to show they could make the hoop swoosh, & the backboard
buckle.

In the summer, concrete was our stadium, & the sidewalk
was our 100-level seats.

In the winter, we slid around like we were playing hockey,
but a cold lob

was safer than catching pucks from a cop's poor pass.

Jordan was king of our broken kingdom,

Pippen was a prince who should've gotten his riches,

& Rodman was treated like some jester,

but this royal court wouldn't have won their last battles

without his swift hands & sharp elbows to the board.

We were once loyal subjects in front of small TVs

who now stare at sacred numbers hanging from rafters.

All due respect to the current stampede.

But we see ghosts of games we could never attend

& cheer our teams who made us feel like champions.

WHEN I THINK OF YOU

I catch your bell jingle in my ear
Summons for a smooth, simple treat
Respite from the scorch of summer,
and the sweat pooling at my feet

I pursue you like hailing a cab
to an unsung destination
Discovering at the end of our ride,
an abundance of variation

Limon, tangy neon sign announcing summer
Strawberry like the red flush on my cheeks
Tamarindo sours, but quenches, my sharp desert tongue
Chocolate like the eyes of the boy I'm in Love with

You're always a reliable friend for those few months
when the city thaws and climbs out of its slumber
Frosty, solid, and two-dimensional, your sturdy sticks
disguise a taste bud tornado bursting from my lips

Your simple flavors delight children and adults alike
Reminding us of small joys that relieve a day burdened
by the humidity of the hood, the stickiness of the streets
Emerging as the days stretch and put us in a haze,

Paletas, you are so much more than popsicles
You're my abuelita handing me her last dollar.
You're colors of a country that I don't frequent much
You're the fieldworkers that pick the fruit to sculpt you

You're a reminder of ancestors and the connection
to all the flavors they try to assimilate and mass-produce
But they can't replicate this flood of memories
melting what rushes to numb me

WHEN YOUR GIRLS MAKE IT
for Teresa Gonzales

We grew up
In the same hood
Walking parallel streets
Drifting through
The same schools

We assembled dreams
Out of skyscrapers
Flea market knockoffs
Ditching class
And young love

Now our lives are perpendicular
We stroll flawless sidewalks
Leave lipstick on wine glasses
But affection for our hood
Runs through us

Pride in my girls
Is hanging on stoops
House music all night long
Cruising down 18th
Graffiti sparkling walls

We grace the world
With what they discarded
Blossoming
From the palette
In our souls

Everywhere we go
Our Chi-Town accents shine
A resistance against
Those that said
We wouldn't

CHICAGO TO LA TO CHICAGO

A flight attendant on break next to me
eats a sandwich smeared with cream cheese.
She watches Everything Everywhere All At Once
on her iPad, and I wonder how it is
to bounce from city to city.

How it all must be a thrill at first—perhaps.
Then it becomes routine, becomes work.

But as travelers, we're eager for the plane to touch down.
So we can shoot over stars etched into floors.
So we can stuff palm trees in our suitcases; to make it
through snow and seasonal depression
when they sweep in.

Graffiti scrawled on walls and chipped bars
on windows remind us of the heat back home.
Walk into a bookstore on Larchmont Blvd,
and even on vacation, we recognize gentrification.
But it doesn't stop me from searching
for my favorite poets. Still smitten by their language
and line breaks, even if they sit on my shelves in Chicago.

In a bright-blue bakery, sun-kissed faces blur
into sparkle-dusted sand and the overlap chatter
becomes ocean waves. I cradle a chocolate croissant
in my hands. My first love sits across from me, enjoying
the biggest everything bagel I've ever seen.
And it's funny and ironic and funny again.
He, who has been everything to me,
in every poor, sad, sick moment, is here eating
an everything bagel, and it's not one
of those poor, sad, sick moments.

I bask in how we have endured—integrated
all the moments that almost killed us
into this ridiculously lucky moment of bliss.
How ridiculously lucky I feel to float this lightly
in a world cruel like concrete in hundred-degree heat.
How it all feels ridiculously tender. My heart

can't hold it. Never gets stale when it happens.
Never less surprising when I encounter it. How I fall
in love again over hibiscus coconut ice cream, discussion
of my favorite films, and raccoons clinging to backs.

It never gets old, this ridiculous splendor.
My heart brimming with centos, soundtracks
belting out *no one is going to fool around with us.*
Driving up and up narrow streets, amazed at how
different the descent is. How two truths can hold
the same weight. How two places can be adored.

NOTES

FIVE-YEAR-OLD CHILD was written for 5-year-old Jean Carlos Martinez who died after falling ill while living in the temporary migrant shelter located in Chicago's Pilsen neighborhood on Sunday, December 17, 2023.

DREAMING OF THE 'BURBS was written with a line from The Smith's song "There Is a Light That Never Goes Out"

CITY OF BROAD SHOULDERS 2024 is written after Audre Lorde's "New York City 1970" and the title of the poem alludes to a line in Carl Sandbug's poem "Chicago."

In WITCHES & SPIRITS, the "witch hat" is part of the older architecture of some buildings in Chicago. A liquor store on the South Side of the city was deemed a historical monument because part of its roof was a witch's hat.

In MCDONALD'S ON CERMAK AND WESTERN, "fight for fifteen" refers to the campaign for a $15 minimum wage for Chicago workers. Launched in 2012, organizers and workers used protests and strikes, particularly by fast-food workers, to fight for higher wages, union rights, and better working conditions.

In TASTE OF CHICAGO, I write about working the annual summer food festival Taste of Chicago. The festival has been taking place each summer since 1980.

In CHICAGO TO LA TO CHICAGO the last stanza contains a line from "Angeles" by Elliott Smith

ACKNOWLEDGEMENTS

Thanks to the editors of the following journals in which the following poems first appeared, sometimes in slightly different versions.

FIVE-YEAR-OLD CHILD was published in the 2025 summer issue of *Milwaukee Avenue Messenger Vol.1, No. 1.*

SMILE STREET was published in the 2025 summer issue of *Milwaukee Avenue Messenger Vol.1, No. 1.*

A SATURDAY AFTERNOON IN OUR URBAN LANDSCAPE was published in the 12/15/2020 online issue of *The Acentos Review.*

WHEN I THINK OF YOU was published in the 04/15/2021 print issue of *Chicago Reader,* in partnership with the Poetry Foundation.

4 DE JULIO was published in the 09/30/2021 issue of *La Libreta, An Online Journal Presented by Robles Writes*

LA MARIPOSA MONARCA MAKES A LIST OF PLACES TO VISIT IN CHICAGO was published in the 11/2021 print issue of *La Raiz Magazine.*

WHEN YOU GIRLS MAKE IT was published in the 02/02/2023 print issue of *Newcity Magazine.*

WITCHES & SPIRITS was first published as "Witches & Spirits in Chicago" in the 02/2024 print issue of *Pest Control Magazine.*

Huge thanks to Arcana Poetry Press for believing in this collection of poems.

ACKNOWLEDGEMENTS

Thank you to the Frost Conference on Poetry, the Roots.Wounds.Words. fam, Jon Sands and the Emotional Historians community, DreamYard Rad(ical) Poetry Consortium, The Watering Hole, VONA, Tin House Summer Workshop, Pilsen Arts Community House, everyone in the Pilsen community including Willian Guerrero, The Kid From Pilsen, Caroline Watson and Grandma's House Poetry, Los Angeles Poetry Society, and the Chicago Public Library. Many of these poems were first drafted, read, and handled with care by my fellow poets and community members in these spaces.

Special thanks to these poets, creatives, and friends who championed, believed, and supported me in one way or another along this journey: Karla Cordero, Elisabet Velasquez, Kemi Alabi, Bree Bailey, Natalie Balestri, Stephen Energia Gifford-Bell, Mónica Cervantes, Estela Victoria-Cordero, Angelica Julia Dávila, Sylvia Ewing, Derick Gellangarin, c.r. glasgow, Mónica Gomery, Edna Gonzalez, Teresa Gonzales, Nicole Lashawan Junior, Tomasa Moncebaiz, Tania Perez Osuna, Hilesh Patel, Elia Alamillo-Rico, Delia Saucedo, Bri Santina, Suzi Q. Smith, Brenda Vaca, Emma Younger, Ana Zavala. My love to you all.

My eternal appreciation and love to my sister Lucy, the Franco, Hernandez, Rodriguez, and Arellano families, my beloved Rolando, and mi hija Iliana. I wouldn't have gotten here without your love and support.

Rocío Franco is a Chicana poet born and raised in Chicago. She holds fellowships from The Watering Hole, Roots Wounds Words, and Periplus Collective. The following organizations have supported her work: the Frost Place, The Lighthouse Writer's Workshop, VONA, and Tin House's Summer Workshop. She is a two-time Best of the Net and Pushcart Prize nominee. Her poems have appeared in *The Acentos Review, Exposition Review, Lunch Ticket, L@tino Literatures Journal, AGNI, December magazine*, and others. You can connect with her work on Instagram @chio_la_chingona.

Photo taken by E.L.A. Photography.

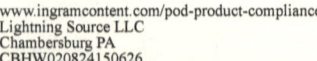